W9-AZW-905

Creepy Creatures

Snails

Monica Hughes

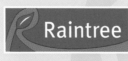

Raintree

Chicago, Illinois

Printed and bound in the United States at Lake Book Manufacturing, Inc.
07 06 05 04
10 9 8 7 6 5 4 3 2

Library of Congress Cataloging-in-Publication Data:
Hughes, Monica.
  Snails / Monica Hughes.
     p. cm. -- (Creepy creatures)
Includes bibliographical references (p.   ).
Contents: Snails -- Looking for snails -- A snail's body -- A snail's
tentacles -- Snail trails -- Snail eggs -- Food for snails -- Snails in
danger -- Snails in winter -- Types of snails.
  ISBN 1-4109-0625-6 (lib. bdg. : hardcover) -- ISBN 1-4109-0651-5 (pbk.)
  1. Snails--Juvenile literature. [1. Snails.] I. Title. II. Series:
Hughes, Monica. Creepy creatures.
  QL430.4.H848 2003
  594'.3--dc21

                    2003008289

Acknowledgments
The Publishers would like to thank the following for permission to reproduce photographs: p. 7 Heather
Angel; pp. 6, 21 Ardea: John Daniels, p. 19 Steve Hopkin, pp. 12, 22a, 22b, A Weaving; pp. 4/5, 17 BBC
NHU: Juan Manuel Borrero; p. 14 Bruce Coleman: Jane Burton; p. 22c Holt ; p. 16 Natural Visions:
Brian Rogers; p. 13 NHPA: Ant Photo Library, p. 11 Image quest 3D, p. 10 E.A Janes; pp. 15, 18 Oxford
Scientific Films: p. 20 K.G Vock; pp. 8, 9 Robert Harding Picture Library

Cover photograph reproduced with permission of Premaphotos/K.Preston-Mapham

Every effort has been made to contact copyright holders of any material reproduced in this book.
Any omissions will be rectified in subsequent printings if notice is given to the publishers.

Some words are shown in bold, **like this.** You can find out
what they mean by looking in the glossary on page 24.

Contents

Snails

Snails are small animals that live outside.

shell

body

They have soft, slimy bodies and hard shells.

Kinds of Snails

There are many different kinds of snails.

Some snails live on land. Other snails live in water.

Snail Bodies

A snail's body is called a **foot**.

foot

A snail can pull its foot into its shell.

Snail Tentacles

Snails have four **tentacles** on their heads.

Two tentacles taste and smell.

eye
tentacle

tasting and
smelling
tentacle

Two tentacles
have eyes.

11

Snail Trails

Snails move very slowly.
They slide along on trails
of slimy **mucus.**

13

Looking for Snails

Snails live in gardens.

You might find some in a flower pot.

You might find snails in some leaves.

New Snails

New snails **hatch** from round, white eggs.

eggs

Baby snails are very small.

They have soft shells and bodies.

Food for Snails

Snails eat the leaves and flowers of dead plants.